D0874916

We Need More
One Day The Clouds Brought Us Together

We Need More Clouds

Copyright © 2021 Lynnett S. Craig
All Rights Reserved.

The moral rights of the author have been asserted.
ISBN: 979-8-9852246-0-3 Paperback
ISBN: 979-8-9852246-2-7 Hardback
ISBN: 979-8-9852246-1-0 Digital online

Published by We Need More LLC
Brandywine, MD
www.weneedmoreclouds.com

Library of Congress Control Number:
2021922553 and 2021922593
Printed in the United States

Acknowledgments:

To my family, thank you for hanging in there when times are tough. We can weather any storm and still come out on top. A blended family is not easy by any means, but each day we learn how to navigate and be better than the day before.

To my husband, Phil, thank you for believing in my vision and pushing me out of my comfort zone to get things done. I love you! Tre', my favorite son, you came right on time, and our family needed you more than you'll ever know. Continue to be a sweet boy and give Mommy all the kisses. To my daughter, Peyton, you are me personified. You have more courage and take more risks than I ever will, and I will always admire that about you. You are my sunshine, and I love you. To my bonus daughters, Leah and Shaniya, thank you for showing me how to love beyond myself. Leah, your love and electric energy make this family complete. Shaniya, your creativity and love for all things fashion help to shape you, and I can't wait to see your name in lights one day. You are the best big sister around. I love you both!

As my family continues to grow closer, I am thankful for all the good days and the not-so-good days that make us stronger. Thank you, God, for the clouds! It was on a cloudy day that I saw how God was going to save my family. We need more clouds!

In remembrance of:

Shirley Honor Anderson Price

The best example of love, kindness, and grace. She truly loved her
family and showed her love with her gift of cooking.
We will eat kale and chicken, laugh, dance, and rejoice in your
honor. I miss you every day.

Pastor Philip McGuire Wesley, Sr., aka Papi

The most generous, sincere, and witty person I've ever known.
You are missed tremendously. It was my honor to be called your
"daughter."

WE NEED more CLOUDS

By Lynnett S. Wesley
Illustrated by: HH-Pax

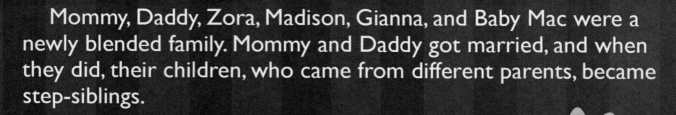

Mommy, Daddy, Zora, Madison, Gianna, and Baby Mac were a newly blended family. Mommy and Daddy got married, and when they did, their children, who came from different parents, became step-siblings.

Mommy had Gianna, who was nine years old. Daddy had Madison and Zora, who were ten and fourteen years old. Together, Mommy and Daddy had Baby Mac, who was just one year old. Mac was the half brother of the three girls, and he was the glue that bonded everyone together.

Mommy was proud of her new family, but she felt they needed to connect more.

The family struggled with time in between visits and physical living distance.

It was tough for Mommy to see how they could form a stronger family bond. Then one day, the phone rang. The family was going on a trip.

It was a very cloudy, hot day in Mt. Dora. The family had just arrived after a long trip to Florida.

But this was no ordinary trip to Florida. The family was there to visit Papi, who was sick.

There were no plans to go to the amusement parks, beach, or swimming pool.

Grand-Mommy bought something fun for the family.

"Surprise, girls!"

"A pool!" Gianna and Madison screamed excitedly. But it was no ordinary pool. It was a huge pool, big enough for the whole family.

Gianna and Madison asked Daddy to blow up their new pool and played in it all day long. Zora talked on her cell phone with her feet kicked up. Baby Mac took a nap while Mommy and Daddy were busy working remotely for their jobs.

After a long day of helping
Grand-Mommy around the house,
Mommy invited everyone to get in the pool.
She thought this would be a great bonding activity.

But all Gianna and
Madison wanted to do was
splash about.

Splish! Splash!

Splash! Splash! Plop!
"Please stop splashing!" Mommy told the two girls.
"Yeah! We just want to relax," Daddy said.

"You girls don't know how to chill," added Zora, the oldest sister.
Gianna and Madison settled down at last.

Papi could hear the family in the pool, which was right outside his bedroom window.

Splish! Splash!
"Yay!" the children shouted.
"Shhh!" Daddy told them.
He was afraid they would disturb Papi from his rest.

Trying to get Baby Mac to sit still was often a challenge for Mommy and Daddy. He got into everything! He was a very curious baby and would laugh hysterically when he got caught putting something in his mouth that he shouldn't.

It was Baby Mac's first time in the pool, and he loved it!

He splashed and kicked with his little hands and feet. Splish! Splash! He even put his head underwater.

Mommy admired the clouds for a few minutes as the family talked and joked here and there in the pool. Something was missing. Mommy asked all the girls about school, summer plans, and their hobbies. She even tried to crack a joke or two, but nothing was working. Everyone was in their own world.

The family had many outings together when Mommy and Daddy dated.

They enjoyed going to amusement parks, the movie theatre, the beach, mini golf, and international trips. Some of their favorite trips were long rides in the car.

But when Mommy and Daddy got married, something seemed to change.

Mommy asked all the girls and even Daddy to put their devices away. She declared it a "no-device zone."
Being in the pool like this gave the family a chance to relax together with no interruptions.

Being a newly blended family had its challenges, and being in the pool was just what they needed. Everyone could be themselves, and no one was trying to outdo one another. No one could go off in the corner by themselves. Daddy made a few jokes while everyone watched Baby Mac splash in the water.

As they sat in the pool, Mommy looked up and saw the clouds moving at a rapid pace.

Finally, Mommy said, "Look up! What do y'all see?"

Madison shouted, "I see a bear!"
Gianna yelled, "I see a bunny!"
Zora said, "I see a train."
Daddy studied the clouds. "I see a boat."

Mommy saw an image of her grandmother Shirley in the clouds, but she kept that to herself.

More clouds rolled in. Gianna, Madison, and Zora quickly pointed the images out.

"I see a cat," Gianna said.
"Look! There's a baby like Baby Mac," Madison said.
Zora pointed out a butterfly and a purse.

Mommy said, "There's Mickey!"
"Can we go to the amusement park?" the girls all asked at once.
Mommy and Daddy shook their heads.
They were there to help Grand-Mommy with Papi.
All the girls made sad faces for a minute, but they understood.

As they continued to look at the clouds,
Gianna said, "I see a dog."
"I found a cruise ship," said Madison.
Zora said, "There's a frog."
There were so many images in the clouds.
The family couldn't name them fast enough before
they changed shape.

There were also images in the clouds that one person would see that the others couldn't quite make out.

Daddy said, "Hey, I see my pickup truck—" He quickly stopped in the middle of his sentence, as the shape had already changed. The family laughed as they called out more images they saw.

"I see myself in the pickup truck!" Daddy said.
"Where?" everyone else yelled. The whole family laughed again.
"We don't see what you see," Zora said.
"Just use your imagination," Mommy said, and everyone laughed.

As Mommy sat there, she closed her eyes and began to praise God for the moment they were sharing. Everyone was happy, smiling, and eagerly anticipating more clouds passing by. They were a family.

It did not matter if they were a blended family. They were one family. Laughter and making memories together was what made them whole.

As the clouds began to move and the images drifted away, Mommy wished for more clouds. She didn't want their time together to end.

10 Essential Steps

to create a Happy Blended Family

- Acknowledge the challenge.
- Come up with a plan.
- Try walking in your kids' shoes.
- Remember that change is never easy.
- Be aware and respect your kids' experience.
- Recognize and praise each family member's achievements.
- Provide the validation your child needs—affirmations go a long way.
- Create a personal relationship with your bonus child(ren).
- Be specific about your needs.
- Keep in mind that everyone's feelings are different.

Made in the USA
Middletown, DE
13 May 2022

65734020R00015